HEALTHY FOOD CHOICES

Snacks

Vic Parker

Heinemann
LIBRARY
Chicago, Illinois

Edited by Rebecca Rissman, Dan Nunn, and
    Diyan Leake
Designed by Philippa Jenkins
Original illustrations © Capstone Global
    Library Ltd 2014
Picture research by Tracy Cummins
Production by Helen McCreath
Originated by Capstone Global Library Ltd
Printed and bound in China

17 16 15 14 13
10 9 8 7 6 5 4 3 2 1

Library of Congress Cataloging-in-Publication Data
Parker, Victoria, author.
    Snacks / Vic Parker.
        pages cm.—(Healthy food choices)
    Summary: "Read Snacks to learn how to make healthy
food choices at snack time. Different photos show
healthy and unhealthy snack options, while simple text
explains why some choices are better than others. A
snack foods quiz concludes the book."—Provided by
publisher.
    Includes bibliographical references and index.
    ISBN 978-1-4329-9119-7 (hb)—ISBN 978-1-4329-
9124-1 (pb) 1. Nutrition—Juvenile literature. 2.
Snack foods—Juvenile literature. 3. Health—Juvenile
literature. I. Title.
    TX355.P255 2014
    613.2—dc23   2013015692

Acknowledgments
We would like to thank the following for permission
to reproduce photographs: Capstone Publishers
(Karon Dubke) pp. 4, 7, 8, 9, 10, 11, 12, 13, 14,
15, 16, 17, 18, 19, 20, 21, 22, 23, 24, 25, 26, 27;
ChooseMyPlate.gov p. 29 (with thanks to USDA's
Center for Nutrition Policy and Promotion; Shutterstock
pp. 5 (© Diego Cervo), 6 (© Shestakoff).

Cover photograph of chopped vegetables and sauce
on a plate reproduced with permission of Shutterstock
(© Africa Studio) and crisps reproduced with permission
of Shutterstock (© valzan).

Every effort has been made to contact copyright
holders of material reproduced in this book. Any
omissions will be rectified in subsequent printings if
notice is given to the publisher.

All the Internet addresses (URLs) given in this book were
valid at the time of going to press. However, due to the
dynamic nature of the Internet, some addresses may
have changed, or sites may have changed or ceased to
exist since publication. While the author and publisher
regret any inconvenience this may cause readers, no
responsibility for any such changes can be accepted by
either the author or the publisher.

Contents

> Some words are shown in bold, **like this.** You can find out what they mean by looking in the glossary.

Why Make Healthy Choices?

Food is fuel for our bodies. We need food in order to think, move, and grow. To work properly, our bodies need different kinds of foods, in the right amounts for our age and size.

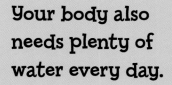

Your body also needs plenty of water every day.

Making the right choices helps you stay healthy and happy.

Eating the right foods helps you to feel healthy and have lots of energy. It helps you think quickly and clearly. It helps you look your best, too.

What Makes a Snack Healthy or Unhealthy?

Eating a snack is a good way to keep up your energy between meals. However, some snacks are much less healthy than others. For instance, salty snacks such as chips are high in **sodium**, which is bad for your heart.

High-sugar snacks can give you **tooth decay**.

The amount of calories in a food is usually written on its packaging.

2 chocolate cookies
around 300 calories

1 orange
around 100 calories

The energy food gives us is measured in **calories**. You need a certain amount of calories per day to stay healthy, depending on your age, your size, and how active you are. If you eat too many calories, you may become **overweight**. If you eat too few, you may become too thin.

Fruit

Fruit is very good for you. However, **processed** fruit snacks often contain unhealthy added ingredients. Extra sugar adds **calories** but does not make the snacks filling. **Artificial additives** such as **flavoring, coloring,** and **preservatives** are **chemicals** that have few **nutrients** and can even be harmful.

added sugar

added artificial coloring, flavoring, and preservatives

Some processed fruit snacks are more like candy than fruit.

bananas

apple

grapes

melon

pear

blueberries

pineapple

orange

strawberries

Eating different colored fruits gives you a healthy variety of vitamins and minerals.

Fresh fruit is a healthier choice. It contains natural sugar, which gives you energy. Fruit is packed with **vitamins**, **minerals**, and **antioxidants**. Your body can use these to grow, repair itself, and resist illness. Fruit also has lots of **fiber**, which keeps your **digestive system** working properly.

Cheese

Cheese contains **calcium**, which builds strong bones and teeth. However, many cheeses, such as full-fat cheddar, are high in **saturated fat**, which clogs the heart and blood vessels. Cheese can also be high in **sodium** and **calories**.

Processed cheese snacks often contain artificial **flavoring**, **coloring**, and **preservatives**.

cheese dippers

string cheese

low-sodium
cottage cheese

grapes

Low-fat, low-calorie, low-sodium cheeses are a healthy choice. These include feta, mozzarella, low-fat cheddar, and some cottage cheeses. Eat just a small portion, with some fresh fruit for added energy, **vitamins**, **minerals**, and **fiber**.

Cookies

Everyone loves cookies, but they usually contain white flour, which is low in **fiber** and **vitamins**. Cookies are also often high in **saturated fat** and sugar.

sugar

white flour

butter

Cookies are tasty for an occasional treat, but not healthy as an everyday snack.

Homemade oatmeal cookies can be a healthy alternative. Use a recipe with **whole grain** flour, which is high in fiber and vitamins. Use vegetable oil instead of butter and use honey or dried fruit instead of sugar.

vegetable oil

whole grain flour

oat flakes

honey

Homemade oatmeal cookies can be both delicious and healthy.

raisins

Popcorn

Popcorn is kernels of corn that are heated until they puff up and burst. Store-bought popcorn that is coated thickly in sugary or **savory flavorings** can be extremely high in **calories, saturated fat,** and **sodium.**

buttered popcorn

toffee popcorn

salted popcorn

caramel popcorn

chocolate popcorn

cheese popcorn

There are many unhealthy kinds of popcorn.

Balsamic vinegar and cinnamon are tasty, healthy toppings for homemade popcorn.

balsamic vinegar

cinnamon

Popcorn made at home can be very healthy. As a **whole grain** food, it is high in **fiber**. Without coatings, it is low in saturated fat, calories, and sodium. It is also high in **antioxidants**—natural **chemicals** that strengthen your body's ability to fight disease.

Chips

Potatoes can be good for you, but not when they are fried. Potato chips are high in **saturated fat**, **sodium**, and **calories**. Baked, unsalted vegetable chips are healthier, but still not as healthy as fresh vegetables.

Vegetables lose their **nutrients** when they are made into chips. Unhealthy ingredients are added, too.

beet chips

sweet potato chips

parsnip chips

potato chips

carrot chips

Crunchy rice cakes are a healthier choice since they are low in fat and calories. Buy the unflavored type and add your own healthy toppings.

Rice cakes are filling and they stop you from feeling hungry between meals.

cinnamon

hummus

peanut butter

fruit spread

Yogurt

Like cheese, yogurt is a good source of **calcium** for healthy bones and teeth. However, full-fat yogurt is high in **saturated fat**. **Processed** yogurts contain many **artificial additives** that are unhelpful or even harmful to your body.

high in fat

added **flavoring**

added **preservatives**

high in sugar

added **coloring**

There are many unhealthy types of yogurt.

Low-fat natural yogurt is healthy because much of the saturated fat has been taken out and no artificial additives have been put in. This sort of yogurt can help your stomach work properly and can even help your body fight **infection.**

whole grain cereals

Add your own healthy flavorings to natural yogurt.

raisins

nuts

fresh fruit

honey

Dips

Some people think that corn chips are a healthy snack if they are eaten with an avocado or tomato dip. However, corn chips are not much lower in **saturated fat** than potato chips. They are also high in **sodium**.

sour cream

tomato dip

cheese

corn chips

avocado dip

Corn chips are especially unhealthy when they are smothered in high-fat cheese and sour cream, as nachos.

It is much healthier to eat vegetables, instead of corn chips, with dips. Dips made at home from fresh ingredients are healthier than store-bought ones, which can contain **artificial additives** such as **coloring** and **preservatives**.

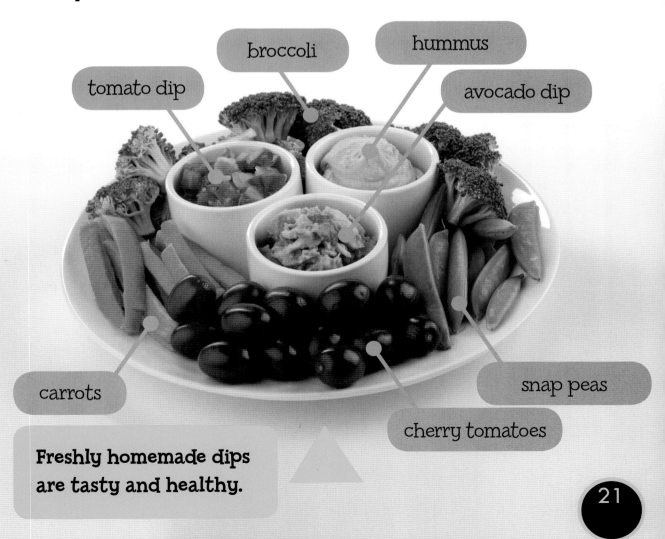

broccoli

hummus

tomato dip

avocado dip

carrots

snap peas

cherry tomatoes

Freshly homemade dips are tasty and healthy.

Sweet Treats

Although many of us find chocolate delicious, it is usually made with added milk and sugar, which means that it is high in fat and **calories**. Also, milk and white chocolate contain little or no healthy **fiber**.

milk chocolate

white chocolate

Milk and white chocolate are not filling snacks.

If you crave a sweet treat, try a banana or dried fruit. These are packed with natural sugar. Eat just a few squares of dark chocolate made with more than 70 percent **cocoa solids,** as this has less fat and sugar than milk or white chocolate and contains a little fiber.

The healthiest chocolate choice is dark chocolate that contains fruit or nuts, for added **vitamins** and **minerals.**

banana

raisins

prunes

dark chocolate

dried cranberries

apricots

Drinks

Milkshakes contain **calcium** for strong bones and teeth, and **protein** for healthy skin and muscles. Smoothies are packed with **vitamins** and **minerals**. However, milkshakes are also high in fat, and smoothies can be high in sugar. This makes them both high-**calorie** drinks.

milk, ice cream, whipped cream, sugary sprinkles

fruit **concentrate**, added syrup, sugar, sweetened yogurt

Milkshakes and smoothies can contain more calories than some desserts.

Water is the best drink at snack time. You can mistake thirst for hunger, so if you drink water, you may not need a snack at all. Also, your body loses water all the time, so you need to replace it to stay healthy.

Flavor water with slices of fresh fruit.

ice

orange

lemon

lime

water

Food Quiz

Take a look at these snacks. Can you figure out which picture shows unhealthy snacks and which shows healthy snacks, and why?

water

raw mixed nuts

fresh blueberries

The answer is on the next page.

soda

blueberry muffin

pretzels

Food Quiz Answers

These are the healthy snacks. The mixed raw nuts and blueberries are packed with **fiber**, **vitamins**, and **minerals**. They are also high in energy, but low in **sodium**. Every part of your body needs water to work properly.

These are the unhealthy snacks. The pretzels will give you energy, but they are high in sodium. The blueberry muffin is high in **saturated fat** and sugar and low in fiber and vitamins. The soda is high in sugar and **artificial additives** such as **coloring** and **flavoring**. Did you guess correctly?

Tips for Healthy Eating

Use this MyPlate plate guide to choose the right amounts of different foods for good health. Choose low-fat cooking methods and do not add salt (it is high in **sodium**). Don't forget to drink several glasses of water and exercise every day.

ChooseMyPlate.gov

See if you can get the right balance over the course of a whole day.

Glossary

antioxidant substance that helps your body fight off disease

artificial additive human-made substance that is added to food, such as coloring, flavoring, and preservatives

calcium mineral your body needs to build strong bones and teeth. Calcium is found in dairy foods and some vegetables, nuts, and seeds.

calorie unit we use for measuring energy

chemical substance made by mixing other substances together

cocoa solid chocolate that has had the cocoa butter taken out

coloring something added to food to make it look attractive

concentrate juice that has had most of the water taken out so that it lasts longer

digestive system all the body parts that break down food so the body can use it

fiber part of certain plants that passes through your body without being broken down. This helps other foods to pass through your stomach, too.

flavoring something added to food to make it taste better

infection disease caused by germs

mineral natural substance, such as iron, that is essential for health

nutrient substance in food that is good for your body, such as vitamins, minerals, and antioxidants

overweight heavier than is healthy for your age and size

preservative something added to food to make it last longer

processed made or prepared in a factory. Processed foods often contain artificial additives.

protein natural substance that our bodies need to build skin, muscle, and other tissues. Protein is found in foods such as meat, fish, and beans.

saturated fat type of fat found in butter, fatty cuts of meat, cheese, and cream. It is bad for your heart and blood.

savory having a salty or spicy, rather than sweet, taste

sodium natural substance found in salt

tooth decay problem when the outer layers of the teeth are dissolved away

vitamin natural substance that is essential for good health

whole grain made with every part of the grain, without removing any of the inner or outer parts

Find Out More

Books

Malam, John. *Grow Your Own Snack* (Grow It Yourself!)
   Chicago: Heinemann Library, 2012.
Parker, Vic. *All About Fruit* (Food Zone). Irvine, Calif.: QEB, 2009.
Veitch, Catherine. *A Balanced Diet* (Healthy Eating with
   MyPlate). Chicago: Heinemann Library, 2012.

Internet sites

Facthound offers a safe, fun way to find Internet sites related to this book. All of the sites on Facthound have been researched by our staff.

Here's all you do:
Visit **www.facthound.com**
Type in this code: 9781432991197

Index